TIMBER IN THE
WORKING FOREST

Mary A Livingston   **Tim Livingston**

Mary A Livingston

RedTail Publishing
Anderson, CA, U.S.A.

Red Tail Publishing

Established 1993

P.O. Box 1477, Anderson, CA 96007
www.redtail.com

Timber in the Working Forest

Paperback ISBN13: 978-1-941950-09-8

Also available in ebook.

facebook.com/TimberWorkingForest
facebook.com/RedTailPublishing

To Beautiful,
Sunshine,
and Mister Man,
may you always enjoy
the wonders of nature.

Contents

Chapter One
Tat-a-Tat-Pat

Tat-a-tat-pat. Woodpeckers gobble up fetal beetle bugs.

Tat-a-tat-pat.

Tat-a-tat-pat.

The overgrown forest is abuzz with activity.

The firs and pines crowd
side-by-side where wormy grubs
hide inside. Insects feast and
spread disease in the stressed
tightly squeezed trees.

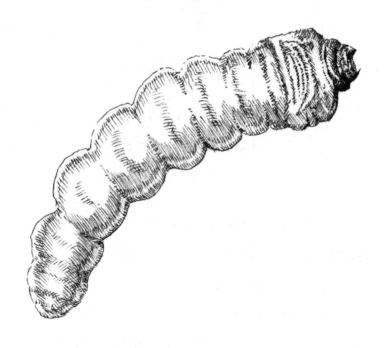

Beastly bark beetles
munch a brunch of tasty
cambium crunch.

Unaware of nature's
need, visitors move in, out,
and about the forest.

Chapter Two
Whirrrrrr-Irrrrrr
Boop-Boop-Boop

A wildlife biologist tunes her radio.

Whirrrrrr-irrrrrr-boop-boop-boop.

She spots a fisher dashing over a log.

She counts all critters in burrows and trees. Where they live and rest their head. When they play and how they're fed.

Whether abundant or few,
she makes a special note if
they have babies brand new.

Chapter Three
Scratch, Scrape, and Sift

An archaeologist finds human artifacts with a scratch, scrape, and sift.

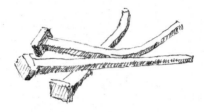

Soil layers reveal hidden midden and other traces left by people working, hunting, and living a long time ago.

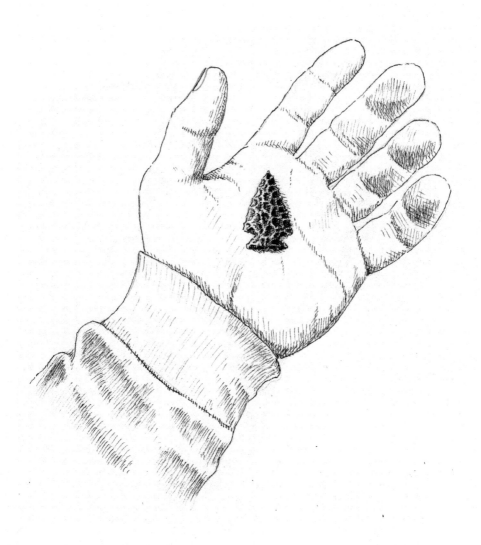

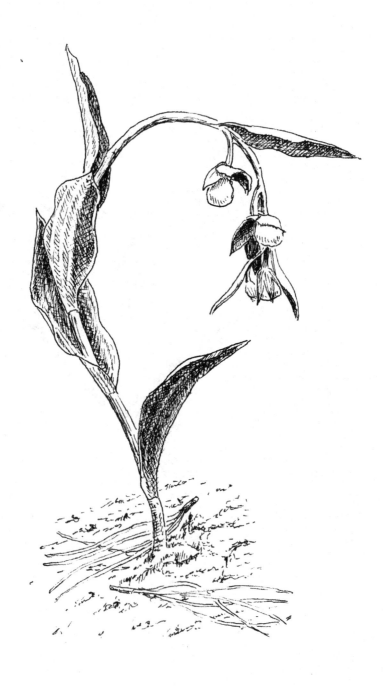

Chapter Four
Woodsy Plants

Botanists survey woodsy plants
on the sensitive list. They guide the
way to treat them right. Some need
shade and some need light.

Foresters count the trees and check the size. A healthy forest is their prize. When they know which seeds to sow, they make a plan to help trees grow.

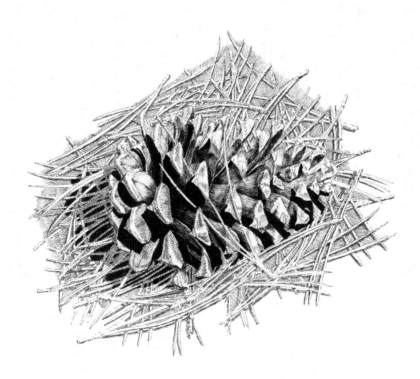

Chapter Five
The Forest Plan

The forest team gathers the history and science of people, animals, plants, soil, water, and trees. As a caretaker, the forester studies all of these.

A little thinning is what this forest needs.

Chapter Six
The Harvest

With a snap and wrap of the forester's tape, it's harvest time in the working forest.

Measure and mark the crowded and weak. Size and select for lots of board feet. Some tree marks mean to take. Other marks mean to leave. The wood adds up when tallying tall trees.

Outfitted with boots and snazzy suspender straps, loggers keep safe with hardhats and chaps. They have goggles, gloves, and protective earplugs.

Rhrrrrrrrrrrrrr-rhrrrrrrrrrrrrr.

A faller's chainsaw hums, cutting and bucking.

The feller-buncher's tree-hugging grip keeps the logs coming. Fresh cut trees pile up in oodles of doodles.

Lift, pull. Lift, pull. Again and again.
The skidders drag and the logs roll in.

The landing is a happening place where logs are bucked and processed to length.

The chaser works a speedy pace. *Clank. Thump.* The choker drops.

Rhrrr. Rhrr. The chainsaw grunts. *Rhrrr. Rhrr.* Clean the logs. Bump the knots.

27

With a racked, stacked, and
chained-up load, the logging truck's
ready to hit the road.

Chapter Seven
The Sawmill

At the mill yard, the unloading begins. Then it's *whip-snap* of the scaler's log tape.

Measure and weigh then check for defects. Watch out for bug holes, pitch pockets, and peck. Splits, shake, and stain don't make the grade. Cull the bad logs and take them away.

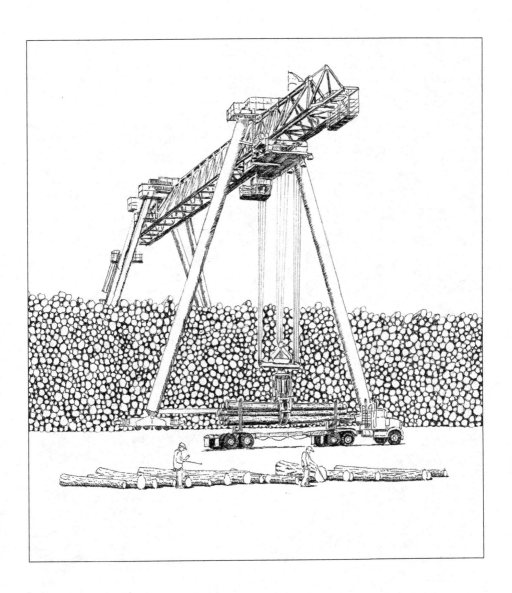

The portal crane lifts, hoisting real
high. Only good logs get decked to
the sky.

In the sawmill, logs are debarked and scanned. A computer maps out the best cutting plan.

The laser-guide shines where the saws slice and dice. *Whirrrrrrrrrrrrrrrr.* One by one, the logs transform into planks, beams, and boards.

Wahhhhh-ahhhhh-ahhhhh-ahhhhh.
Bull wheels whirl and swirl, turning tall
timber. A shaver peels poles from lanky,
long logs. Stacks of new poles fill the
pole yard.

Chapter Eight

Nothing to Waste

They use every piece and part of the log. The bark becomes nuggets to landscape drought friendly yards.

The hungry wood hog grinds leftover scraps. It devours cull logs like a big tasty snack. Chunky chips are sorted for paper pulp and mulch. The rest becomes fuel for power and heat. It's stockpiled in mounds and high rising heaps.

The hopper feeds fuel nonstop to the boiler. The fuelwood churns and

burns, producing high-pressure steam.
Whirling turbines turn out electricity
that's clean. Extra cogeneration
energy helps the community utility.

Chapter Nine
Wood Products

Forklifts pack and stack the train
with racks of lumber. A pole baler
loads the long pole trailer. Milled
wood ships to factories, builders, and
stores.

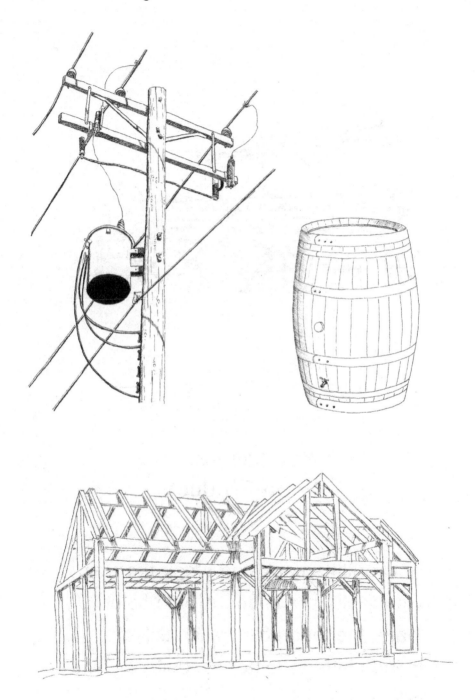

Wonderful wood
becomes homes,
power poles, tables,
books, and toys.

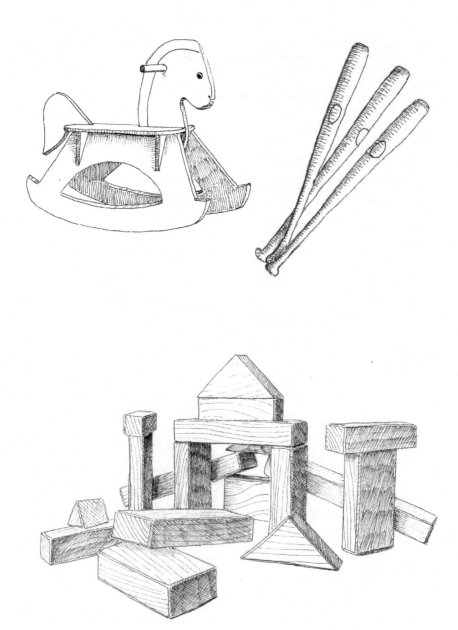

Chapter Ten
Cleanup Crew

Back in the forest, it's time for the cleanup crew. A wood-chipper chews leftover tree tippy-tops. It blasts the woody chips into a waiting chip truck. Cogeneration bound, the trucks haul the chipped hog fuel to town.

Controlled fire, nature's tidy-up
tool, cleans the forest floor removing
slash and debris. Nutritious ash
enriches the forest soil.

Planting grass in a fresh straw
bed keeps the soil from eroding and
washing away.

Chapter Eleven
Scalp. Break. Plant. Pack.

Tree planters arrive with hoedads and full planting bags.

They scrape the soil and make a hole. Into its place, a seedling goes.

Then they pack the soil tightly closed.
The hoedad rhythm fills the hills.
Scalp. Break. Plant. Pack.
Scalp. Break. Plant. Pack.

Where a clear-cut once was,
thousands of new trees grow.

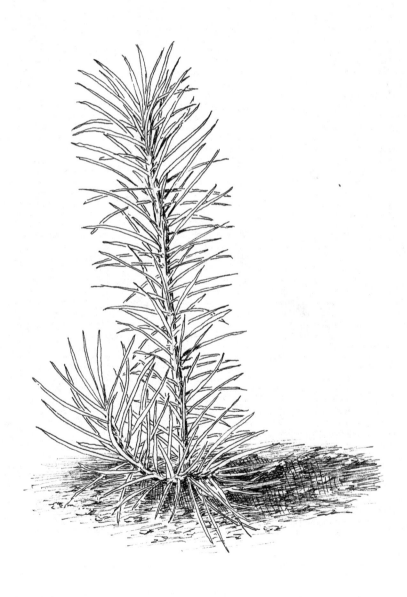

Chapter Twelve

Chit-a-chat Look at That

Slap. Slap. Slap. Mama bear

watches from nearby as her cub

scampers up a pine.

Chit-a-chat. Chit-a-chat.
Squirrels skedaddle up, down, across,
and around. *Chit-a-chat.* Their alarm
sounds.

A wide-eyed child explores
the busy scene.
Look-at-that.
Look-at-that.
The working forest is abuzz
with activity.

Working Forest Extra-Stuff

more about foresters

more about loggers

cogeneration   recycled paper

tree products   glossary

about the author   about the illustrator

Foresters

*Trained professionals
who manage the health of a forest.*

Education
> Foresters receive on the job training
> and/or university education, especially
> in environmental science.

Degree
> Science

Licensing
> Typically a professional license is required for
> writing harvest plans.

Work Habitat
> Most foresters work in the forest and in an office.

cruiser's vest

marking paint

Biltmore stick

logger's tape

diameter tape

Specialties
- Log Buying
- Timber Harvesting
- Logging Engineer
- Forest Planner
- Research
- Inventory
- Reforestation
- Environmental Inspector

Work Activities
Foresters write forest plans, cruise timber, mark trees, and hike many miles.

Temperament
A forester must be willing to work outdoors, alone or with a team, and long hours in all kinds of weather.

Purpose Served to Society
Foresters maintain and improve the environmental health of the forest ecosystem while providing sustainable and affordable wood products.

Loggers

*Skilled professionals
who harvest trees for wood.*

Education
> It takes years of professional training to
> become a skilled logger. Loggers must also
> learn about environmental rules and work
> safety.

Work Habitat
> Forests

Work Activities
> A logger's job is physically demanding. It
> includes hill climbing, problem-solving, following
> the logging plan, cutting trees, bucking logs,
> choker setting, loading and hauling logs. A
> logger starts work at the crack of dawn.

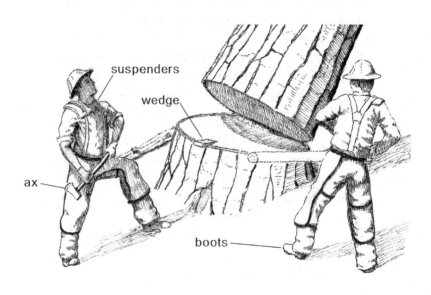

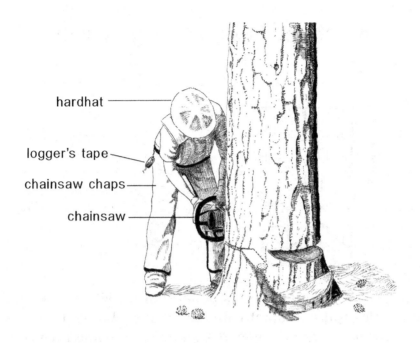

hardhat

logger's tape

chainsaw chaps

chainsaw

Temperament
A strong mind and body with a willingness to work outdoors in both good and bad weather are required.

Specialties

- Pole Logging
- Cable Logging
- Helicopter Logging
- Mechanized Logging
- Salvage Logging

Purpose Served to Society
Loggers provide sustainable and affordable wood products.

A Closer Look at Cogeneration

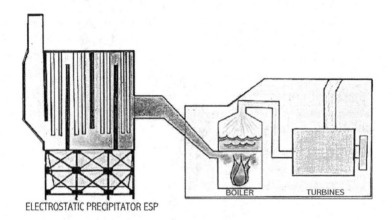

ELECTROSTATIC PRECIPITATOR ESP

BOILER   TURBINES

Wood fueled cogeneration facilities make clean, green electricity and heat by burning wood scraps, chips, branches, and thinned trees. Pages 36-37.

Boiler – Wood scraps, chips, and sawdust are burned in the boiler. The boiler superheats water to a high-temperature, high-pressure steam.

Turbines - Steam from the boiler turns the turbines and generates power. It makes enough electricity to run the mill. Extra electricity is transferred to the power grid for community use.

Heat - Leftover steam from the turbines provides heat. The extra heat transfers to the mill's heating system. Sawmills also use this moist heat to slowly dry lumber so that the wood doesn't crack.

Electrostatic Precipitator (ESP) -

Polluted smoke from the boiler weaves through a maze of positively charged electrode surfaces in the ESP. These electromagnets pull ionized particles from the polluted exhaust like a magnet pulling iron filings from sand. Clean air is released into the atmosphere.

Hair Raising Fun

This fun experiment shows what happens to fine particles like ash when exposed to an electrostatic charge.

Materials:
One balloon
Plate of ash or fine matter
(cornstarch or flour)
Dry head of hair

- Prepare plate with ash or substitute.
- Inflate the balloon to full and tie off.
- Without making any changes to the balloon, Hold the balloon over the plate of ash. Observe.
- Next, rub the balloon on the head of hair until the hair stands on end.
- Then hold the balloon over the ash.
- What happen?

Recycled Paper

Read the instructions in advance. Air temperature and humidity will affect the time it takes for the paper to dry.

Things you'll need:

ADULTS - One is enough for a small group. More for a larger group.

USED PAPER STOCK - Newspaper, egg cartons, paper bags, old homework sheets, or dull printed paper. Don't use glossy paper.

WATER

DISH PAN, SHALLOW PAN or TRAY

PITCHER

SPATULA

FOOD PROCESSOR or MORTAR AND PESTLE

FRAME - Inside measurements equal to paper size.

SCREEN - Outer measurements should be slightly larger than the outside of the frame.

FELT - Two white pieces for each sheet of paper you plan to make. Colored felt may stain paper.

ROLLING PIN

RAG TOWELS

IRON

BAKING COOLING RACK
GELATIN - For sizing the paper.

Step One:

Tear the paper stock into small strips or pieces. Place in a dish with hot water. Soak for at least an hour. Overnight soaking is best. Don't soak in a sink because it'll clog the drain.

Step Two:

Place pulp mixture in a food processor. Pulp that's too dry is hard on the motor, be sure it's wet and soppy. You may also use a mortar and pestle on this step.

Add small amounts of warm water as needed. Blend until relatively smooth. Place blended pulp in dishpan or pitcher. NOT in the sink. Add warm water and stir until soupy.

Optional Step Three:

Sizing keeps the paper from being too porous. If you want to write on the paper, add gelatin at this point or do *Optional Step Eight* later on. Dissolve about a teaspoon (5 ml) of gelatin in one cup (240 ml) of boiling water. Add to pulp mixture.

Step Four:

Place a screen over a dishpan or catch bowl. Place the frame on the screen. Pour some pulp in the frame area.

If you don't have a frame to contain the pulp, pour the pulp in the center of the screen and shape the edges with a spatula.

Option:
Use large, open cookie cutters instead of a frame for fun paper shapes.

Allow the water to drain. Draining time will vary.

Optional Step Five:

While the paper pulp is still wet on the screen, add decorations such as thread, glitter, or leaves.

Step Six:

After most water has dripped from the paper, remove any framing from around the paper mass. Lay a sheet of felt over the paper mass. Turn over onto a hard protected surface. Place second piece of felt over the back side. Roll out excess moisture with the rolling pin. Or press out moisture with your hand. This is a messy step and should be done in an area that is easy to clean.

Step Seven:

Protect the ironing surface with extra newsprint or towels. Keep felt in place, put screen and paper on the ironing surface.

Press with a hot iron. Gently remove the screen after a few passes. Iron paper between felt until desired smoothness.
The paper may also air dry on baking cooling racks before ironing.

Optional Step Eight:

Sizing keeps the paper from being too porous. If you didn't size the paper in *Optional Step Three*, you may add this step. Dissolve a teaspoon of gelatin in one cup of boiling water. Use a shallow 2" (5 cm) tray or pan with 1" (2.5 cm) of water in it. Add boiled solution to water in tray. Dip one sheet at a time. Handle carefully when hot and wet.

Let paper dry.

Botanical Art Bonus Fun

In *Optional Step Five*, use added items such as dried leaves, grass, and flower petals to create a picture in your paper.

Tree Products
A forest gives us many things.

Trees give us more than just paper, lumber, and furniture.

Wood flour, fiber, and resins help make plastics stronger. The organic sugars that make wood strong also help make products strong.

If organic wood sugar is combined with nitric acid or other nitrating agents, it can produce enough power to make rocket fuel.

The liquid left over from making paper is also useful because of its natural stickiness.

Some tree nutrients provide nutritional supplements for humans and animals.

The following list contains some less obvious tree items. People try to use all parts of a log.

acetate

adhesives

ammonia

appliance casings

aromas

baby food

bacterial agents

ballpoint pen tubes

binders for ores, charcoal,
   & animal feed

buttons

carbon paper

cattle supplements

cement

ceramics

cereals

chewing gum

chicken supplements

citrus oils

cleaning compounds

cosmetics

counter tops

cutting oils

deodorizers

detergents
disinfectants
domino tiles
drilling fluids
driveway cleaners
dust abatement
emulsifiers
enamels
essences
eyeglass lenses
fertilizer
fish supplements
floor polishes
floor tiles
fragrances
fungicides
gummed tape
household cleaners
impact resistant additives
improved concrete
insecticides
insulation
irrigation piping
lacquers
laminating adhesives
latex products
lead storage batteries
leather tanning agents
lime scents

medicines for high blood
    pressure & Parkinson's
    disease
molded luggage
molded simulated wood
mylar
odorants
oil varnishes
packaging
paint
paint removers
pet foods
photographic film
photographic paper
plastic tool handles
plastic twine
plastics for toys
preservatives
pressure sensitive
    adhesives
printing inks
rayon
rayon cording for tires
rubber products
sanding sealers
sandwich bags
sausage casings
shampoo
skull reconstruction plates

soaps
soil conditioners
soil erosion controllers
solder fluxes
solvents
sound proofing material
spice oils
spirit varnishes
straws
street lamp shades
tempering oils

thermoplastic molding
toothpaste
torula yeast
turpentine
urethane
vanillin
varnishes
water treatment agents
wood preservatives

Did you know?

Author, Mary A Livingston, has a tree product in her head. Part of her skull had to be replaced. Plastics and resins were combined at the time of surgery to make a skull reconstruction plate that is stronger than her real bone.

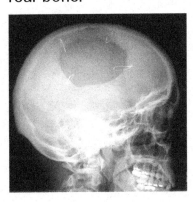

Here's an x-ray image of her head. The tree-resin plate looks **very** different than the bone.

Trees make cool stuff!

Glossary of Terms as used in Timber in the Working Forest

ancient – Something very old from a long time ago.

archaeologist – A person who looks for evidence of people and their culture from a long time ago. Page 11.

artifacts – Ancient items used by people a long time ago, often found by archaeologists. Pages 11-13.

bark beetles – A beetle that burrows beneath the bark to lay its eggs. Page 3.

bark nuggets – A common term for chunks of tree bark used in landscaping as ground cover. Page 35.

Biltmore stick - A tool for cruising timber. It measures the height of a tree and the width of its trunk. A forester uses a Biltmore stick to help calculate the amount of wood in a tree. Pages 18, 56.

board feet – A board foot (BF) is a unit of measure for milled wood. Another unit of measure for wood is cubic meter (m³). Page 20.

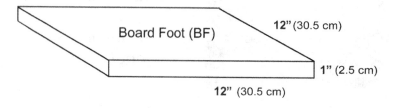

Board Foot (BF)   12" (30.5 cm)

1" (2.5 cm)

12" (30.5 cm)

boiler – A device in a cogenerator for boiling water to generate steam. Pages 36-37.

botanists – A plant expert. Page 15.

bucking – A term for cutting a tree into specific lengths of logs. Pages 24-25, 27.

burrows – Holes in the earth where animals live or sleep. Some animals dig a burrow, others convert a natural crevice.

cambium – The growing layer of a tree right under the bark.

chainsaw – A motorized saw with a toothed chain for cutting wood. Pages 23-25, 27, 58-59.

chaps – A thick protective leg covering worn over pants. Pages 23-24.

chute – A tube-like structure for guiding wood chips. Page 36.

clear-cut – A logging site where most or all of the trees are removed. Pages 46-49.

cogeneration – The use of fuel to produce steam and electricity. Pages 36-37.

controlled fire – The intentional use of fire to clean up woody debris. Pages 44-45.

cull – To sort and remove something with a defect. Also a descriptive word for a defective log. Pages 30, 36.

debark – To remove the bark from a log. Page 33.

decks – Stack logs in an organized pile. Pages 26-27, 31.

defect – A characteristic that makes a log undesirable for lumber or poles.

doodle – A small pile of freshly cut trees. Page 25.

earplug – A safety device to protect hearing.

eroding – The process of wearing or washing away soil.

faller – A person who cuts trees for harvest. Pages 24-25.

feller-buncher – A machine that cuts trees down and bunches the cut trees into a pile called a doodle. Page 25.

fetal beetle bug – Baby beetles also called larvae. Page 2.

forest plan – A plan to take care of the health of a forest.

forester – A trained professional who manages the health of a forest. Pages 16-21, 44-45.

forester's tape – A long, flexible measuring tape a forester uses to check log diameter and length. Page 16.

forklifts –
A tractor with forked prongs for carrying lumber. Page 38.

fuelwood – Woodchips used as fuel in the boiler. Pages 36-37, 43.

grapples – Large mechanical prongs that come together in a pinching motion for picking up logs or gripping tree trucks for cutting. Pages 25-26, 28, 31.

grubs – The worm form (larva) of an insect. Page 2.

hardhats – An impact resistant head covering worn for protection. Pages 23-24, 27-28, 31, 44, 58-59.

harvest – To gather a crop.

hoedad – A long bladed hoe-like
   tool for planting trees.
   Pages 46-48.

hog fuel – Wood scraps
   for use by a chipper
   or wood hog grinding
   machine before being
   used as fuel in a
   cogeneration plant.
   Pages 36-37, 43.

hoedad

landing – A cleared place near the harvest site
   where trees are processed into logs and
   loaded onto trucks. Pages 26-28.

landing chaser – A person who unhooks trees and
   trims them at the landing. Page 27.

laser-guide – A beam of highly intense light used
   to guide machines with exact precision.
   Pages 32-33.

leave tree – A tree marked with paint that won't be
   cut during harvest.

limbing – Removing the branches of a cut tree.
   Page 24.

loader – A machine with tines or grapples used
   sort and load logs; also a machine with a
   bucket to load chips; any machine used to
   carry and load a product.
   Pages 28, 30, 36-37, 39.

logger – A person who manufactures logs.
   Pages 22-28, 58-59.

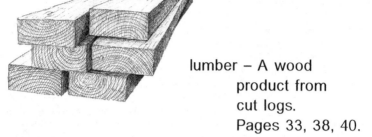

lumber – A wood
    product from
    cut logs.
    Pages 33, 38, 40.

midden – Layers in the soil that have traces of
    ancient human activity. Page 12.

overgrown – Trees in a crowded state where
    there's not enough water, sunlight, and
    nutrients to sustain them. Page 18.

paper pulp – Softened wood fiber in a mushy form
    for making paper. Pages 62-66.

pitch pocket – A cavity in a log filled with pitch

pole – A long slender log made from a tree with
    the bark peeled off.
    Pages 35, 39-40.

pole baler – A loader designed to haul long logs
    known as poles. Page 39.

sawmill – A place for processing logs into lumber.
    Pages 30-39.

scaler – A person who measures and estimates
    how much lumber is in logs. Pages 30-31.

scaler's log tape – A long, flexible measuring tape
    a scaler uses to check log size.

scalp – The act of removing the top organic layer
    from the soil before planting trees.

seedling – The first stage of a young tree.

seedling   sapling   pole   mature tree

old-growth   snag

sensitive list – A set of plants or animals that have special habitat requirements to live.

shake – Annular ring separation in a defective log.

shaver – A machine used to peel away the bark and outer layer of a log to make a pole. Page 34.

skidder – A tractor with grapples for pulling logs to a landing. Page 26.

slash and debris – Branches, twigs, and bark left after harvest. Small amounts of slash and debris helps the soil. Too much raises the fuel load and fire danger. Pages 43-45.

splits – A defect in a log exhibited by a linear crack along its length.

stain – A defect in a log causing permanent discoloration.

suspenders – Straps worn over the shoulder to hold pants up. Pages 23-24, 58-59.

take tree – A tree marked for cutting during harvest.

tally – The act of counting and adding.

thinning – To remove some trees to ease crowding.

turbines – A fast spinning motor powered by steam that generates electricity.

wildlife biologist – A professional who is an expert on wild animals. Page 6.

wood hog – A machine for grinding wood scraps. Page 36.

woodsy plants – Plants found in the wooded forest.

About the Author

A Gelett Burgess Children's Book Award recipient and California Federation of Chaparral Poets honoree, Mary, grew up in the forested communities of Humboldt and Trinity Counties of Northern California. She has worked in photography, education, publishing, and liturgical design.

Her career in children's literature focuses on nature and environmental education. Mary's outdoor life activities of wildlife photography, hunting, gardening, gold mining, and rock hounding keep her close to nature. She and her husband, Tim, have two sons and three grandchildren.

www.maryalivingston.com

About the Illustrator

A Registered Professional Forester, Tim works and lives in rural Northern California. His career in natural resources spans over 40 years. He considers his forestry career an awesome job and likes that his desk is the hood of his truck and the trees in the forest his office walls. His love of the outdoors includes wildlife photography, hunting, gardening, gold mining, and rock hounding.

As an artist, he started as most with a set of crayons. Then in his teens, comic books increased his interest in creating art. Watercolor is his favorite artistic media followed closely by pen and ink and photography. Tim draws on his extensive forestry experience for accuracy in his art.

www.theforesterartist.com